ALL ABOUT SLOTS
AND
VIDEO POKER!

John Gollehon

A PERIGEE BOOK

A Perigee Book
Published by The Berkley Publishing Group
200 Madison Avenue
New York, New York 10016

First Perigee Edition 1988

The Putnam Berkley World Wide Web site address is
http://www.berkley.com

PHOTO CREDITS:
Front cover: Bally Manufacturing Co., and International Game
Technology (IGT). Back cover: *Mechanical* — Bally's 4-reel, single
payline, "ghost" machine accepting from 1 to 3 nickels. Note the
large jackpot for the third coin! *Video* — IGT's popular "Fortune
Multiple Bonus," a 4-reel, 3-payline machine that pays both left to
right and right to left. This machine is usually found in million-
dollar progressive carousels.

Library of Congress Cataloging-in-Publication Data

Gollehon, John. T.
    All about slots and video poker! / John Gollehon. — 1st
Perigee ed. — New York, NY : Perigee Books, 1988, c1985.
        p.   cm.
    ISBN 0-399-51458-9
    1. Slot machines.   I. Title.
    TJ1570.G57   1988
    795.2—dc19   88-12503
                                                        CIP 4/88

Printed in the United States of America

25   24   23   22   21   20   19   18   17   16   15

CONTENTS

The author wishes to express his appreciation
to the following companies for providing
assistance and information:
Bally Manufacturing Co.
International Game Technology (IGT)
Mead Publishing Corporation
The Desert Inn, hotel and casino
Las Vegas Convention and Visitors Authority
Nevada Gaming Commission
Nevada Gaming Control Board
New Jersey Casino Control Commission

CHAPTER 1

WHAT YOU NEED TO KNOW ABOUT SLOTS

It's surprising what most slot players know about slot machines.

Not much.

Unfortunately, the same can be said for other casino games as well: most blackjack players know little about card-counting; most crapshooters can't identify the good and bad bets; and most roulette players don't realize that the casino's edge against them is so solidly and mathematically entrenched.

But the slot players have an excuse. In fact, their excuse is the main reason they play. Most players believe they have nothing to really learn about! There are no strategies to memorize like at blackjack, and no complicated table layout to contend with like craps. It's simple. If you can find the coin slot... and the handle... you're in business.

Some "expert" slot players I've talked to can't understand why anyone would write a book about playing slots.

1

Or why anyone would bother reading it. Everyone knows how! Right?

Wrong!

That contention couldn't be farther from the truth. Such reasoning probably helps to explain the considerable player losses, and big casino gains. Slots are the casino's biggest money-maker. And it's not difficult to see why.

All About Slots is not the first book on slot machines. Nor the last. Indeed, there's a wealth of material available, or perhaps "glut" is a better word. In fact, one of the prime purposes of this book is to weed through some of the other literature available, sorting out the good and the bad advice. And believe me, I've found bad (and dangerous) advice in what would appear to be authoritative works. The last thing you need is wrong or questionable advice, especially since you're playing with real money. *Your* money!

All About Slots will give it to you straight. No hype. No funny stuff. You'll know exactly what your chances really are to win. You'll be able to select the right machines that can provide a better opportunity. You'll realize a fresh, smart, and broader understanding that should, at the very least, enrich your enjoyment of playing.

That's what *All About Slots* really is. Now, let me tell you what *All About Slots* isn't. It's not a carrot-on-a-stick luring you through the pages in the hopes of finding some radical new strategy, or sure-fire system that will help you relieve the casino of thousands of dollars. There is no such system. There is no such strategy.

I'm a firm believer in giving my readers the real bottom line. Slots are indeed fun to play, and sure, you might get lucky and hit a jackpot in the thousands, maybe millions. The real attraction of slots is obvious. For a relatively small investment, as little as three dollars, you could conceivably win over a million dollars. But you must understand that *no one can play exclusively for profit*. The only regularity of profit belongs to the casino. Over the long period, the odds are astronomical that you will come out ahead. But then again, you probably already know that.

Authors claiming in bold headlines that you can learn "how to win," with even a fair degree of consistency, are plainly out to lunch. It's a "sucker" approach, and the authors must assume you've just left the farm for the very first time. Frankly, you should resent that.

The very best any author can do for a slot enthusiast is to increase the player's educational awareness. Ideally, this realistic approach will help to minimize player losses, and hopefully increase the likelihood, however small, of hitting substantial jackpots. An important part of this approach is to identify and dismiss all the foolhardy notions that confuse or perhaps jeopardize the beginning player.

If it's possible to define a "skilled" slot player, and if indeed, a player can actually be skilled, the definitions would have to include: the ability to recognize the basic variations among machines; an interest (and patience) to best determine the frequency of payouts; a full understanding of player options; and most important of all, a generous application of sensible money-management and old-fashioned discipline. These are the very things that we will cover in detail on our way to becoming a better player.

In order to chart this course as smoothly and simply as possible, I've elected to concentrate on only the machines that are presently in use in most casinos. You won't find any data on antique machines or other historical facts. For the majority of players, there's little interest in vintage machines. They want to know about the machines they'll find in the casino *today*. Sure, there are thousands of collectors of antique slot machines; it's a fascinating and enlightening field. If that's your main interest, pick up a book on antique slots. But be careful. Collecting old slot machines is against the law in several states, and they are not cheap! Collecting, like playing, can become downright addictive!*

Another area that we'll avoid is inside the machines. Many slot purists believe that the better player must understand all the aspects of the machine's internal parts. No thank you. If you don't have a graduate degree in electrical or mechanical engineering, don't worry about it... because I don't either.

The purist's belief is rubbish. When you learn how to use a computer, is it really that important that you learn about integrated circuits, silicon chips, and microprocessors? Of course not. When you purchase an automobile, is it necessary to tear inside the engine? Some do I suppose, but for most people, the assumption that internal workings are properly designed and installed, engineered expertly, securely, and safely is all that really counts.

With slot machines, you may correctly assume that they have been designed and improved over the years to insure an unwavering random process and will not cheat you. Anything more than that is really not important. For most of us, learning how to play and having fun with slots is well within our grasp. Leave the high-tech stuff to guys with scientific calculators, mechanical pencils, and clip-on rulers in their shirt pockets.

Before we study the variations among slot machines, let's first find out if slot machines are really worth playing. Are slot players wise, or are they foolish?

To accurately answer that important question, and to rate slots among the other casino games, we first must understand percentages, because that's what it all boils down to.

---

*The author recommends the following sources for readers who are interested in antique slot machines: 1) Mead Publishing Corp., 21176 So. Alameda St., Long Beach, CA 90810, publishers of *Loose Change* Magazine and many excellent books on slots; 2) Gambler's Book Club, 630 S. 11th St., Las Vegas, NV 89101, an established retail bookstore (and mail-order house) carrying a large stock of books and articles on gambling; 3) Atlantic City News Agency, 101 S. Illinois Ave., Atlantic City, NJ 08401, a good source for gambling books out East.

CHAPTER 2

THE CASINO ADVANTAGE

If the casino pays off your winning bet with an amount that's something less than the true probability of winning that bet, then they have acquired an advantage. It's usually expressed as a percentage. A percentage that applies to every single bet you make. A percentage that over a *long-term* period of plays, will always prove out.

In short-term play, a few hours or so, virtually anything is possible, unless the percentage is unusually high. A player at the slot machines or at the table games, in a very short time period, can realize great profits or lose heavily, regardless of the percentages. Remember that just about anything can happen when tested over a shortened period of trials.

We'll look at percentages more closely in a later chapter, but for now, learn the simple terms that are used when talking about percentages. Each time you pull the handle, your bet is called a "trial" or "event." And any variations in the outcome from the correct probabilities are called "fluctuations" or "deviations in probability." Probabilities are

often expressed as a ratio such as 10 to 1 odds. Accordingly, "probability" means the same as "odds." And from
time to time, we'll refer to the casino percentage as the
"casino advantage." It means the same.

Understanding the important difference between long-
term and short-term play is also essential to this discussion.
Rarely will a player gamble for a few hours, and then quit
for life. For the great majority of players, gambling is one
short session after another. And they add up. They add up
to a long-term exposure where the greatest likelihood of
these nagging percentages can eat you alive. *No matter how
small the percentage against you, the longer you play, the
more likely you will lose.*

So, in short-term play, fluctuations from the norm are
more likely to occur. Hopefully, all the fluctuations will
happen in your favor, one jackpot after another. But don't
be so naive as to think that you can't possibly pump $20
into a slot machine without a single jackpot, big or small.
It can happen, and if you play often enough, it will happen frequently. Be prepared for negative swings in deviat-
tion and cut them off with quick action. Quit!

When talking about percentages, the casino refers to it
as "hold." And so shall we. **In Atlantic City, the New Jersey
Casino Control Commission has established regulations
that require all casinos to return at least 83% to the player.**
Simple arithmetic tells us that the hold percentage must be
17% or better. So, if the hold is indeed 17%, **over the long
term** you can expect to lose $17 for every $100 you risk.

**In Nevada however, there is no regulation that specifies
a minimum return to the player or maximum hold percentage for the casino.** Technically, Nevada casinos are free to
set the percentages of their machines as they please. The
Nevada Gaming Commission does require however that all
slot machines have a jackpot of any stated amount that can
be won. If the machine doesn't have a payout of some value,

then it's not considered a gambling device and couldn't be approved for use. How nice. At least you know you won't be face to face with a machine that never pays out.

Well, as it turns out, the spirit of free competition accomplishes the same thing as stringent regulations. In order to survive in such a competitive marketplace as Nevada, the casinos generally provide "decent" hold percentages. It doesn't take long for players to become suspicious of high percentages, and when the word gets out, that greedy casino will be as lonely as the Maytag repairman.

Don't be overly concerned about the freedom of Nevada casinos to set the percentage arbitrarily. In some cases, it works out to the benefit of the player. Remember the days when there were four gas stations on every corner, and the gas wars that would flare up from this intense competition? Today, there aren't many cases of four stations on a corner, but there are casinos clustered and cramped into congested centers of legalized gambling. Sometimes, the casino's marquee tells the story. "We Return 97% on Slots!"

Unfortunately, most casinos do not publicize their hold percentages on slots, and it's difficult for a player to know exactly what the hold really is for a particular machine or a particular casino. A selected number of shrewd slot players know how to obtain at least some measure of input about percentages, on their own, if the casino won't oblige them. We'll cover this important facet of slot play later on in another chapter.

NEVADA PERCENTAGES

In Nevada, it's generally agreed that the hold percentages among the major casinos range from 15% to 3%. Machines with huge jackpots are generally set at a median percentage, and you must understand that if the machines in that group (called a carousel) are to pay off million dollar jackpots, the overall percentage will take that critical factor into account. The casino wants that particular machine to pay off at a determined percentage, *inclusive* of the large, progressive jackpots. Generally, you'll find less smaller jackpots in trade-off for the chance to hit the big one. If we take the large jackpot out of the reach of the player — and for all but absolute certainty we should, then the machine percentage will skyrocket against the player.

There are several Nevada casinos that cater primarily to slot players, and to the locals who live in the area. It's a widely accepted notion that these particular casinos serve up a lower percentage on their machines as compared to the other casinos who rely heavily on table-games and high rollers. Although there's no hard evidence to support that conclusion, it probably has merit. Generally speaking, it would make more sense to play where slot machines provide a greater share of the casino's business, but it's not a hard and fast rule.

Similarly, another general assumption is that slot machines in drug stores or bars, anywhere not associated with big-time casinos, produce higher income for the owners and the least attractive percentages for the players. Again, with little proof to substantiate that statement, there's no firm answer, but the generality sounds darn good to me. I certainly wouldn't play where I have to wait for a guy to bag some groceries before he can pay off my jackpot.

Most all slot machines today are designed to track the total dollar volume of play (called "handle") and the total dollar volume of payouts. The difference represents the casino's hold and is presented in both dollar volume and as a percentage of the handle. In many cases, the slot machines generate this information instantly to a central computer for a print-out on a regular basis.

I recently had a chance to review a casino's print-out for a one-week period noting that the percentage, in consideration of all the machines, was 10.6%. Not surprisingly, this percentage does not vary by more than a few tenths of a percent each week, unless there are extraordinary circumstances.

If the casino has set their machines for an aggregate 10% hold, you can be assured that after an extended period, with all the fluctuations, 10% is exactly what the slot machines, and the computer, will give them.

It's my understanding that this particular casino offers a mix of machine percentages from 15% to 5%, not unlike most other casinos. So, for the sake of argument, let's use the slot machine hold as 10% to compare with the hold of the other games.

ARE SLOTS REALLY WORTH PLAYING?

Most gamblers know that the best game in the casino (for the player who's willing to make a serious effort) is blackjack. In fact, if a player can master a basic strategy, develop an effective card-counting scheme, and find optimum playing conditions, it's possible that the percentage of advantage will actually belong to the player! Of course, for most players, blackjack proves to be a losing proposition, giving away nearly 5% or more through inexperience and ineffective play.

Both craps and baccarat have relatively low casino advantages, depending on the wager, some as low as only 1/2%. Unfortunately, few players make only the lower percentage bets, and wind up giving the casino a fat 3-5% return for their money.

Roulette is perhaps the best example of a purely random game with a constant negative expectancy that defies the player's skill or inexperience. It makes little difference if you know how to play or not. Roulette gives the casino a 5.26% advantage, and you can set your watch by it.

The worst game in the casino is Keno, with a varying

degree of house advantage that can exceed 25%. No respectable gambler would be caught dead in a keno parlor.

So, using 10% for our number, it would appear that all the other games except Keno would be far better to play. But what if we know, or have good reason to believe, that a particular machine is holding only 5%? Then, for the average player who is not an expert at craps or blackjack (nor wishes to risk the large minimum bet at baccarat) the slot machine is not that bad after all! And, if we can find a machine that does indeed return 97% to the player, that particular machine fares strongly against the other games and might warrant play. As you can appreciate, the trick is finding the machine with the lowest percentage.

I should mention here that I'm not encouraging you to gamble, at slots or any other game. The decision to gamble is personal, and must take into account your financial, emotional, and psychological well-being. *There's always a risk, and there are no guarantees.* Give it serious thought before you begin.

Now that we've determined that certain slots are really not that bad — in terms of percentages, there are other factors that favor the machines.

For one, slots are the only casino game where you can end up on easy street for a minimal investment. No other game offers such big jackpots without substantial risk. For another, table-games might conjure up feelings of apprehension and intimidation for some players. The slots on the other hand, are intimate and personal. There's no one watching you at a table, or criticizing your play. The romanticism with slot machines is an age-old tradition. And for most players, it's just plain fun! That important factor certainly can't be discounted.

High rollers consider slot machines about as much fun as sitting around watching paint dry. For others, the slots are just as much fun as a hot crap table, without the complexing nature. My primary game is blackjack but no matter what game I play, if I'm not having fun I won't continue. That element has to be there.

At the beginning of this section, I asked the question, "Are slot players wise, or are they foolish?" These previous paragraphs were to solve that question.

I can't tell you that playing any gambling device with a constant negative expectancy, whether it's 15% or even 1%, is wise. It could be concluded that the blackjack player who has mastered the game is the only "wise" player in the casino. But are slots really "foolish"? I suppose not, especially if you make the effort to play only the low percentage machines, maintain a strict control on your losses, and enjoy yourself along the way. There's nothing foolish about having fun, as long as it's legal, and won't put your marriage in jeopardy. And sure, you can always consider slots as a "cost of entertainment" although I don't particularly like that approach because it has a negative connotation. When you play, it's important that you have prepared yourself for a losing session, but at the same time, you must try to condition yourself in a winning frame of mind. You can't psyche out the machines, but you can psyche out yourself.

To insure that you have fun, be careful not to let losses ruin it for you. **Set your limit, and budget your investment.** Of course, some nice big jackpots make it a lot more fun to play! So now let's look at how we can improve our chances of winning. Let's learn more about the machines themselves.

CHAPTER 3

BASIC "PAY-LINE" VARIATIONS

A few decades ago, the slot machine was pretty standard. The machines were purely mechanical with no electrical systems. Generally, only a single pay-line was offered, and only a single coin was accepted. Jackpots were measured in the hundreds, not thousands, and certainly not millions of dollars, as they are today.

The modern slot machine has advanced through space-age computer technology to become the casino's most high-tech game. There are several variations in basic machine designs which have become more or less standard in the industry. An astute slot player should learn these basic differences and be able to identify the machine's type, and its method of play.

Today, there are three basic styles of reel-type slot machines: the single pay-line, multiple pay-line, and option-buy. In virtually all cases, the machines are multiple-coin, and it's important that you understand exactly what the additional coins buy for you.

SINGLE PAY-LINE

For most single pay-line machines, additional coins will simply increase the payoff of any win. The second coin will double the payoff, the third coin will triple the payoff, and so on. Most often, single pay-line machines will accept either 3 or 5 coins. For example, a typical, 3-reel, single pay-line machine accepting up to 5 quarters will have a pay scale for the jackpot of: 200 coins for the first coin inserted, 400 coins for the second coin, 600 coins for the third coin, 800 coins for the fourth coin, and 1,000 coins for the fifth coin.

But some machines that look similar, might pay off the jackpot at lesser values such as: 100 coins for the first coin inserted, 200 coins for the second coin and so on. The player should not immediately think that the first machine is better, because the second machine might include more smaller wins for a greater number of symbols. Perhaps the machine that appears to be better only pays on 7's, bars, and cherries. But the other machine includes additional fruit that could more than make up for the apparent shortage on the big jackpot.

Equally important, some machines offer the jackpot at a higher multiplier for the last coin. For example, this same basic machine we're describing might pay off 2,000 coins on the fifth coin inserted, instead of 1,000 coins. Always be sure to play the maximum number of coins the machine will accept, especially when the jackpot includes this extra bonus!

All single pay-line machines can be easily identified by the words: "ALL PAYS ON CENTERLINE."

MULTIPLE PAY-LINE

For most multiple-line machines, additional coins will

simply increase the number of lines in play *for the same pay scale*. Generally, multiple-line machines are either 3 or 5 lines, accepting either 3 or 5 coins respectively. The first coin inserted into a 3-line machine will activate the centerline. The second coin activates the top line, and the third coin activates the bottom line. With three coins inserted, you have three lines in play. Any winning combination on any of the three lines will pay off.

The 5-line machine is the same as a 3-line machine except that the fourth and fifth coins allow you to play the diagonal lines from the top left of the top line to the bottom right of the bottom line, and from the top right of the top line to the bottom left of the bottom line.

The slot machine usually has a line inscribed on the glass, or a pictorial description on the "feature glass" above the machine, to fully detail the lines that you can play. Most always, the machine's jackpot can only be won on the last line the machine offers (on the third or fifth coin) and sometimes this jackpot is more than the multiple of coins inserted, so always play the maximum number of coins the machine will accept. In other words, play all the lines!

To assure yourself that you have in fact activated all the lines, look for the line to light up on the feature glass above the machine or look for the indication near the actual pay-line. This is important because sometimes the machine will not register your coin-drop. A malfunction is no excuse to the casino. If the line is not lit and the machine does not show that the final coin was accepted, you won't be paid on that line. Period. Be careful. There's nothing more frustrating than to see a winning combination appear on a line that you didn't buy.

OPTION-BUY

The "option-buy" slot machine features a single pay-line and generally accepts 1 to 3 coins. Instead of increasing a payoff or increasing the number of lines, additional coins merely buy the player more symbols to use for winning combinations. For example, a typical machine might offer only cherries as the winning payoffs for the first coin. The second coin will activate bars, and the third coin will activate the jackpot symbols (usually 7's). As always, if you elect to play only one coin, you take the risk of seeing a jackpot total before your eyes without bells ringing and coins dropping. With option-buy machines, always be sure you have all the symbols activated.

Now that we've learned the "basic" differences among slot machines, we're by no means finished. There are more variations that deal primarily with the display and mechanism, the coin values, and the jackpot amounts. On we go.

CHAPTER 4

THE VIDEO SLOT MACHINE

All slot machines today have mechanisms and displays of three primary types: mechanical, microprocessor-controlled mechanical, and video.

The mechanical slot machine was the work-horse through the casino's growth years in the 1960's. Actual reels spinning in their housing controlled by mechanical devices — the way most slot players still prefer. But these "DC-3's" of the casino industry are giving way to the "jumbo jets" — the most sophisticated, secure, esoteric designs that feature CRT video screens, microprocessors, computer logic, and random access generators that can be programmed in any of over 4,000 different modes (percentages).

And to make the whole thing more complicated, the manufacturers today are building mechanical machines with microprocessors inside to control the mechanical reels. Yes, some machines might look mechanical, but in reality they're wolves in sheep's clothing. Inside are the same silicon chips and integrated circuits that drive the video machines.

And that's not all. Some manufacturers are providing casinos with a "kit" if you will, to convert the old mechanicals to the new generation of computer-controlled slots. That favorite old slot you like to play that sounds mechanical today, might buzz and hum tomorrow. Expect to see many mechanical machines in your favorite casino with the guts of a computer. That's an important issue when our discussion of percentages comes up in a later chapter.

Video slot machines are easy to recognize. A 13" television screen provides a simulation of spinning reels, creates a lot of cute noises, and displays cute little phrases on the screen like... "I'm loose as a goose!" Experienced slot players, for the most part, don't like video machines, but that's another matter. In the years ahead, it will be interesting to see if the manufacturers, the casinos, or the players determine the slot machine's destiny. Will the mechanicals fade away? Will all slots be video?

Since most gamblers are cynical, somewhat distrusting of machines they don't understand, the reluctance to accept this new generation of slots is understandable. Some players are concerned about the incredible complexity of video machines, and the underlying fear of high-tech manipulation. For the old-timers, the change alone is what's upsetting. Was there anything really wrong with the good ol' mechanicals?

Slot machine manufacturers have tried every trick in the book to make the video machines look like and feel like the real thing. Some machines actually show the reels backing up when you begin to pull the handle, just like a real slot machine. Others provide the sounds of the reels "clicking" into position. Still others are attempting to put the mechanical "feel" into the video handle.

Despite the fact that many players prefer the mechanical machines, most casino executives and slot machine manufacturers contend that the video machine represents the future. In most any other business, the old adage about giving the customer what the customer wants holds true. In this case, however, it looks like a "force play" is about to ensue.

The most important issue here however is the "fairness" aspect of the video machine, not the conjecture of its place in the future. Any concern that the video machine could easily cheat the player is unfounded. In consideration of who's operating the machines, and the casino license on the wall, cheating the player is an inconceivable enemy. Especially in the case of the major casino-hotels, the player stands a more likely chance of falling out of an airplane.

Remember that most all casinos can generate substantial income honestly. There's absolutely no reason to cheat. The only instance I can think of involving a slot cheating scam against the player, with the knowledge of management, happened years ago in Northern Nevada. Upon discovery, the Nevada Gaming Commission revoked the casino's license and the operation was completely shut down.

Perhaps the deciding factor in the video slot's future is the positive aspect of its accuracy and reportability to the casino. All video machines, and the microprocessor-controlled mechanicals, are usually connected to a central computer, providing immediate reports on the machine's performance, activity, and condition.

The casino will know instantly if there's a malfunction, an undesirable performance in terms of the set percentage, and for that matter, exactly how the machine has profited for the casino in terms of handle (all bets), hold (the casino's winnings), and percentage. More so, the casino can tell if the machine has been altered, opened, tampered, or tilted. If the machine has been opened, the computer will identify the pass-card holder (a magnetic card is required for access) and monitor the machine closely while open and vulnerable. If a jackpot hits, the computer will alert the casino instantly, and later determine if the jackpot was legitimate.

As you can see, the computer-controlled slot machines are a friend to both the casino and the player.

As the new generation of slot player emerges, raised on video arcades and electronic games, the battle between the mechanicals and the videos will be more or less academic. For the seasoned slot player however, it appears the micro-processor-controlled "mechanical" machines we talked about earlier will be their only saving grace.

CHAPTER 5

THE JACKPOT

Perhaps the most significant variation among slot machines is the jackpot. Again, there are three basic types: standard (non-progressive), double individual progressive, and multiple-progressive.

The standard machine pays a fixed jackpot amount that is clearly posted on the feature-glass of the machine. Most often, the standard jackpots are stated in the number of coins to be won. Sometimes a dollar amount is given. If you're playing a quarter machine with a jackpot of "1,000," be sure you know whether you're playing for 1,000 coins ($250) or a thousand dollars!

The standard machine generally provides a more realistic chance for the player to win the jackpot. Accordingly, the jackpots are not as huge as the ones you read about in the papers. Nonetheless, we'll learn later in this chapter that playing these fixed jackpot machines might be a better move for the player than the million-dollar progressives. The player's odds of winning a jackpot has to be considered in determining which machine to play. Although odds of 8,000 to 1 seem high, such odds are considerably more realistic than 8,000,000 to 1! Later on we'll see how your chances of winning the really big jackpots should be considered as a "hold" percentage against you, along with the casino's normal hold percentage that represents their profit.

Of course, if you're the type of player who can't get excited about the chances of winning a $200 jackpot, your greed is going to cost you dearly. A successful casino player, whether at the slots or at the blackjack tables, must learn how to be happy with a win of any amount. Winning always beats losing, and frankly, winning at all in the casino today is not that easy. Be thankful.

"PROGRESSIVE" SLOT MACHINES

In order to provide larger jackpots, playing on the gambler's greed, the casinos have developed the popular "individual double progressive" machine that pays an ever-increasing jackpot amount depending on the amount of play. The jackpot might reach high proportions in comparison with the same machine without the progressive jackpot feature.

The term "individual" means that the escalating jackpot is based solely on activity of that particular machine, and not affected by other machines nearby. As more and more coins are pumped into the machine, the progressive jackpot increases by a small, fixed amount per wager. The jackpot continues to grow until a lucky player lines up the right combination.

The term "double" means that the machine offers two distinct jackpots, both displayed on a lighted meter at the top of the machine. Usually, a red arrow will signal the jackpot amount that is in effect for each handle pull. The arrow alternates between jackpots with each coin inserted. Most progressive machines in the casino that operate individually have double jackpots.

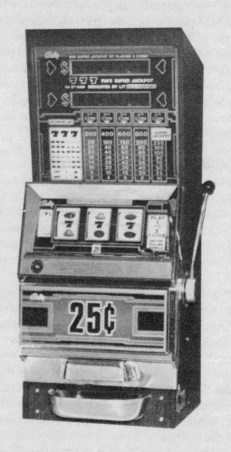

Bally microprocessor-controlled, double individual progressive, single payline, 3-reel, 5-coin machine.

It's common sense for the player to look for individual progressives with the highest jackpot totals (on both meters), since the *amount* of the jackpots has no bearing on the percentage of hold. As in all cases, the casino's percentage of hold is always based on the probabilities of a machine over a long-term, averaged period, *inclusive of the jackpots* that probably will occur based on the odds of that event happening over tens of thousands, maybe hundreds of thousands of trials. The casino relies on the law of averages. It hasn't failed them yet.

Million-Dollar Progressives

Sometimes progressive machines are "banked" together in what the casino calls a "carousel." Unlike the individual progressives, the carousel of machines all contribute to a single progressive meter, brightly displayed above the carousel for everyone to see. These special machines are called "multiple-progressive," and provide the slot player with a chance to win hundreds of thousands, even millions of dollars. The temptation of a "7-figure" jackpot is hard to resist.

Surprising to most players, these machines give the casino their biggest profits, in spite of the huge payoffs.

There's much confusion over the percentages of these high-paying progressives, and most players assume that the casino must hold a high percentage in order to pay off the big jackpot winner. But it isn't so. You must understand that the casino does not pay the jackpot out of their hold percentages (profit). If the casino's hold on the million-dollar progressives is 10% (a likely number), then over a long term of play the casino will have made 10% of all coins inserted as profit, *after* the big jackpot has been awarded! The casino's actual hold takes into account all jackpots, including the biggie.

A popular notion among frequent slot players is to avoid

the million-dollar progressives because . . . "you have to pay too much." In a; sense, that's right. But let's look at *who* you're paying.

LARGEST PROGRESSIVE JACKPOT WINNINGS

AMOUNT	HOTEL	LOCATION	DATE
$2,500,000	Harrah's	Lake Tahoe	1983
2,200,000	Tropicana	Atlantic City	1985
1,500,000	Caesar's	Atlantic City	1984
1,300,000	Golden Nugget	Atlantic City	1984
1,236,319	Harrah's	Atlantic City	1983
1,065,358	Caesar's Palace	Las Vegas	1983
1,000,000	Sands	Atlantic City	1983
1,000,000	Stardust	Las Vegas	1984
385,000	Hilton	Las Vegas	1982
385,000	Flamingo	Las Vegas	1982

This list only includes those casinos that were willing to report directly to us in time for our June 1985 publication. It should not be considered as complete. We accept no responsibility for accuracy or omissions. This list is only intended to show the reader that large jackpots are becoming widespread among more and more casinos every day.

For example, the Flamingo Hilton in Las Vegas reported to us that a $250,000 jackpot was hit *five times* during a three-month period in 1985!

A common practice in many casinos with the big-money carousels is to remove 10% of the handle (all money wagered) each day and place this money in an escrow account. The casino is not saving the money for themselves; it's certainly not their profit! The casino is in fact saving the money for the ultimate winner! This 10% escrow hold has nothing to do with the casino's regular hold percentage that we've estimated for this example to be 10%. In addition to the 10% "hold" in escrow for the eventual winner, the casino continues to earn it's regular 10% "profit" hold.

So, the player in reality is faced with a 20% hold against him assuming that he won't win the ultimate jackpot —

which for all intents and purposes is a logical assumption. The odds are almost beyond comprehension!

Getting back to the notion we quoted, ". . . avoid the million-dollar progressives because you have to pay too much," let's finish that statement. You have to pay too much to the casino, *and* to the ultimate winner! It's your money, and all the other player's money, that pay the big winner. The casino doesn't pay the winner, you do. All of you do.

Technically, it's not entirely fair (mathematically) to "revise" the hold percentage of these machines taking into account the 10% or so of the handle that goes to the winner, and considering it as a hold against all the players. Together, that 10% along with the casino's profit percentage of 10% totals 20%, and that's not the least bit attractive.

But in the case of the giant jackpots, it *should be* revised because your chances of winning the jackpot are slim and none. It's a virtual certainty that you won't make it. For the other machines with more sensible jackpots and far better odds of winning, then we must consider that jackpot as a real probability for us, and weigh only the casino's actual hold against us.

Incidentally, the casino makes big profits on million-dollar carousels not because they turn up the percentages, but because these machines receive so much play. Heavy action! Regardless of the actual percentages against us — and it might be better than 10%, maybe 5% or even 3%, the casinos are the consistent winners.

Another interesting facet of the big progressive jackpots is the short-term unpredictability of winning it. You'll recall from the first chapter that short-term play can result in wide fluctuations from what the true probabilities call for. It's true for the player, but it's also true for the casino! Two or three big wins within a short time-frame, however remote, might raise havoc in the casino's accounting department. If such wins did occur before the casino was able to set aside a substantial escrow, then the casino might indeed pay the winners from their own earnings.

Another factor that the casino worries about is the initial vulnerability after a jackpot has been awarded, depending on the amount the casino sets on the meter to begin the next jackpot. In some cases, the casino might actually be taking some mathematical risk.

CHAPTER 6

MORE VARIATIONS TO LOOK FOR

All video machines are either reel slots, poker, blackjack, or keno. Technically, when a player refers to a video slot, he's talking about the reel-type, not one of the other games. Most likely, the distinction is because the video slot has a handle. And all slots are suppose to have handles, not buttons. Most slot players refer to video poker machines as . . . well, poker machines, not slots.

We've already discussed video slots, and will devote an entire chapter to poker machines. There's little doubt among the experts that poker machines have become the fastest growing casino game. And there's a lot to be said about them.

The "21" machines (blackjack) are also relatively popular, allowing the inexperienced blackjack player to cut his teeth against a machine instead of a real dealer. The rules are basically the same as with the live game, but of course the betting is limited and the excitement is not nearly the same as at the tables.

IGT *Player's Edge* ''21'' machine features a single deck (shuffled after 30 to 40 cards), and offers ''double down'' on 10 or 11. Winnings accumulate on a credit meter, allowing the player to wager up to 100 coins. The player may receive the winnings by pushing the ''cash out'' button. Unlike the table game, this machine awards 1,250 coins for 4 aces in the player's hand only, with 5 or more coins played. IGT offers this machine with four different percentages from 88% to 97%.

Video keno has not received the same degree of acceptance, and accordingly will not be detailed in this text.

There are still two major types of machine variations that we haven't yet covered. For one, all slots accept different coin values. In most casinos, you'll find either 5^c, 10^c, 25^c, 50^c, and $1 machines. Of these values, the 25^c and $1 machines are by far the most popular. In a later chapter, we'll learn that there might be a relationship between the coin value and the casino's percentage of hold.

NUMBER OF MACHINES BASED ON COIN VALUE

HOTEL	LOCATION	5¢	10¢	25¢	50¢	$1
Stardust	Las Vegas	262	32	534	34	222
Landmark	Las Vegas	161	5	386	0	84
Sands	Atlantic City	76	0	1,000	118	243
Harrah's	Atlantic City	67	45	726	188	303
Golden Nugget	Atlantic City	63	0	788	67	284
Caesar's	Atlantic City	84	0	989	182	332

This chart is based on data supplied to us from casinos who responded to our written survey. The numbers should help the reader in determining the frequency of machines now in use. It can be seen from the chart that the 25¢ machines are by far the most popular, followed by the $1 machines.

In some casinos that cater heavily to slot players, you might find that nickel machines are still the most popular. No responsibility is assumed for errors or omissions.

In determining percentages, one of the most important variations in slot machines is the number of reels (and the number of positions on each reel). The positions are called "stops." In the casino, you'll find basically 3-reel, 4-reel, and 5-reel machines. Since this variation relates more to percentages, we'll cover reels and stops in our next chapter.

Slot machines, whether video or mechanical, offer an array of symbols that usually relate to the size of the payoff. The smallest jackpots are generally cherries, followed by the other fruits: lemons, plums, oranges, and watermelons.

Bells and stars indicate moderate payoffs generally, and represent the oldest symbols on the machines. The higher payoffs including jackpots are usually reserved for bars, 7's, or the casino's logo. If the machine uses bars in the payoff scale, generally single bars are lowest, double bars are next, followed by triple bars for the largest jackpot. In some cases, a machine will offer a payoff for any combination of bars: single, double, or triple.

With all the variations among slot machines, it's not surprising to learn that there are exceptions to almost every rule. For example: some machines pay from the left to right only. Others pay from both the left to right, and right to left. Some machines have spaces in place of symbols that casinos call "ghosts." Some machines will accept 9 coins, some more. Some machines have more than one display on the screen, as if the player is playing more than one machine on one screen. There are big machines and little machines; stand-up machines and table-machines. There are games that don't even resemble a slot machine, but look more like an arcade game ... winning dollars instead of points.

The list goes on and on. Understand that the basic differences we've learned are more or less relative, not absolute. Above all, always read the instructions on the machine you wish to play, *before* you play.

CHAPTER 7

UNDERSTANDING PERCENTAGES

The percentages associated with all slot machines are based on what the manufacturers call reel-strips. Although the video machines are based on the same principle, it's easier to understand the concept of "programming" percentages if we consider the mechanical machine with actual reels inside.

As you know, most slot machines feature either 3, 4, or 5 reels. And each reel has a position at which the machine will stop. At the expense of a buzz-word, the manufacturers refer to these positions as "stops."

Now we have the ingredients to determine the frequency of payouts — *the number of reels and the number of stops per reel*. It's really that simple.

The best way to grasp the probabilities of different stops on the reel lining up with identical stops on another reel is to use a coin-flip as an example. Let's say we want to find out the odds of "heads" coming up three times in a row.

First, we have to determine the number of all possible outcomes (probabilities). And to do this, all we need to perform is a simple calculation of multiplying the number of probabilities for each trial, times the number of probabilities for the next trial, times the number of probabilities for the next trial, and so on.

For all you mathematical geniuses out there, you can see that if the number of probabilities is the same for each trial, we simply raise the number by the power of the number of trials (an exponent).

In the case of the coin-flip, there are obviously only two probabilities for each trial — heads or tails. For you smart alecks, we're not going to consider the chance of the coin landing on its edge!

So, in the case of three coin-flips (three trials), the total number of probabilities is: 2 x 2 x 2 = 8. Eight different ways that the coin will come up in three trials. Since we know that heads will come up three times in a row only once out of these eight probabilities, the odds of doing it should be expressed as 7 to 1. Not 8 to 1. The first number in our odds expression represents the number of times the event won't happen. The second number represents the number of times it will. The total of both numbers is the total number of all possibilities.

If you're a football bettor, and you guess at the selections like we all do, your chances of winning three out of three games is 7 to 1. Not so good! Surprised?

OK, we're not going to the casino to flip coins or bet football games. Let's get back to the slots.

If there are 20 different stops on the first reel of a 3-reel machine, you can be assured there will be 20 on the second reel, and 20 on the third reel. If it just so happens that only *one* "7" (our jackpot symbol) appears on each reel, what are the odds of hitting that jackpot?

Simply multiply 20 x 20 x 20 = 8,000. There are 8,000 different combinations that can come up, but only one combination is our 7-7-7. So the odds are: 7,999 to 1. And if you think that's bad . . .

With 4 reels, it's a staggering 159,999 to 1! With 5 reels, (are you sitting down?) it's 3,199,999 to 1!

To really comprehend the severity of these odds, let's compare the chances of hitting the 5-reel, 20-stop machine to getting struck by lightning. The odds are about the same! Now, if it just so happens that in the course of your lifetime, you've been struck not once but twice, I suggest you hurry off to Las Vegas, find a casino, and get some change. See if you're really that lucky. But don't stand under a Palm tree!

THE BIGGER THE JACKPOT, THE GREATER THE ODDS

In order for casinos to offer large jackpots, in the hundreds of thousands of dollars, it's necessary to make the odds of hitting that jackpot even more remote.

So, to accommodate the casino's demand, the slot machine manufacturers have developed reels with more stops — 22 and sometimes 25 per reel. If you really want to know the odds on a 5-reel machine with 25 stops, it's 9,765,624 to 1.

But you must realize that the odds have to be that great in order to provide the chance for a super-jackpot. There has to be that kind of relationship between the odds and the jackpot amount. Otherwise, the casino simply couldn't afford it.

In the case of the video machines which are based on reels and stops that really don't exist, a microprocessor stores all the information necessary to simulate the reels and stops. Since it's all done on a "chip," the programmers can produce as many as 255 stops per reel. I'm not even going to bother figuring out the odds.

Until recently, most video slots were limited to 84 stops per reel, so to increase the odds for a giant jackpot, only the number of reels could be increased.

But today, slot machine manufacturers can utilize a new

chip that provides an incredible 255 stops per reel! So, if you see an easy-looking 3-reel machine with an unusually high jackpot, forget 84 and think 255. Think 255 x 255 x 255, and then consider another machine.

Let's get back to earth by discussing briefly the smaller payouts, like cherries. On a basic 20-stop, 3-reel machine, there might be 7 cherries on the first reel, 7 cherries on the second reel, and 4 cherries on the third reel. The odds of lining up 3 cherries is: $7 \times 7 \times 4 = 196$ chances of appearing out of 8,000 combinations = 7,804 to 196 = 40 to 1. I can live with those odds! Out of 41 pulls, you should receive one three-cherry payoff. But don't expect a million dollars. In line with the odds, you'll receive a modest payoff at best.

"ADJUSTING" THE PERCENTAGES

The slot manufacturers "adjust" the percentage of a machine by considering all the possible combinations and all the possible payouts including the jackpot. If you play the machine one coin at a time for 8,000 plays, and if the game was fair (no advantage for casino or player), you should expect to receive back 8,000 coins in winnings.

But of course the game isn't fair, and the machine will probably not give you back the full 8,000 coins, at least not over long-term play. The number of coins the machine holds divided by the total number of possible combinations represents the casino's percentage (the advantage against you). If, for example, the machine was set to return 7,200 coins over 8,000 pulls, the casino will hold 800 coins. 800 divided by 8,000 is 10%. And that's the casino's advantage — 10%.

The slot manufacturers have two ways to set the percentage. They can design the reel-strips as they please with any arbitrary number of symbols, and they can adjust the payscale that you see displayed on the machine's glass. **The frequency of symbols on the reel-strip, number of stops,** number of reels, and the schedule of payouts, *together* control the machine's percentage.

"Ghost" Machines

Usually, each stop on a reel-strip is represented by a symbol; a cherry, lemon, bars, or whatever. But in some cases, the stop position might have no symbol at all. Stops that are void of any symbol are called "ghosts." Today, you'll find many of these machines in the casino, although a lot of players don't like them. Generally, ghost machines have fewer pay combinations, but they are generally larger. A ghost machine is not necessarily a higher percentage than the others, contrary to popular belief. The "ghost" feature has no bearing on the percentages, so don't hesitate to play it for that reason.

PICKING THE PERCENTAGES

Invariably, a slot machine's percentage is established at the factory based on the instructions of the casino as noted on their purchase order. *Forget the notion that a casino can adjust a screw or turn a hidden knob to change the percentages.* Mechanical machines require a great deal of work to change a percentage, and the newer video machines require a skilled technician. Most often, the casino knows what they want and what they are doing beforehand; rarely is a change required after installation.

The slot machine industry uses a term to describe the success of any machine — "attract mode." It is this factor based on "player appeal" and the equally important term, "stay mode," that determines if a machine has found its home. Percentages are rarely changed to make a machine more popular. The machine must have some "commercial" attraction to lure the player, and a relatively satisfactory payout to retain the player. Indeed, slot machines today are more attractive than ever before, with cosmetic consideration as if designed on Madison Avenue. You'll find bright, lively colors, flashing lights, audio gimmicks, and video messages that beckon the passers-by. Today's slot machines are as hard to resist as ever.

IDENTIFYING THE PERCENTAGES

Although there are no sure ways to determine a reel-slot's actual percentage, I strongly recommend that you *monitor your own play* to determine the percentage as best you can.

Begin with a determined amount of money and let your winnings accumulate in the coin-tray. Play only your original stake, not your winnings! Then, when your initial money is gone, count your winnings. You can easily tell if your "win" is 90%, or 80% or hopefully 120% or more of your original money. You'll be checking frequently over short-term play where, as you know, the fluctuations can be significant. Always keep a record. If the percentage appears to be too steep, move on, or quit.

Always look for advertised hold percentages on the casino's marquee or in newspaper ads in the local papers. If a casino is promoting 97% return on slots, go for it. When you get inside, if you find that the slot machines identified as 97% turn out to be only eight to ten machines, and all being played, then leave at once. Don't let the casino "bait and switch" you! Your guess on the other machines is as good as mine. Stay away!

In Nevada, downtown Las Vegas casinos generally offer better percentages but we can't be absolutely sure in all cases. When I play slots, I prefer to play in a casino that caters primarily to slot players, provided it's not some dump.

In the next chapter, we'll learn that poker machines, unlike reel-slots, offer the player a chance to literally shop for percentages. The player can base the percentages on the feature-glass pay schedule right on the machine, and not worry about what's inside!

CHAPTER 8

VIDEO POKER MACHINES

Video poker machines were first introduced to the gaming public in 1976, receiving a rather luke-warm reception. Although Bally Manufacturing Co. gets credit for the initial debut, International Game Technology (IGT) entered the market in 1978 with resounding success, and deserves the lion's share of the credit for pioneering the machine's acceptance. Today, poker machines are taking more and more floor space in the casino, receiving play from over 25% of all slot players, according to a visitor's profile-study commissioned by the Las Vegas Convention and Visitors Authority. That percentage is expected to increase dramatically over the next few years. The 1984 report also indicated that 10% of all visitors played poker machines. That figure is more than keno, more than roulette, and even exceeds craps! There's no doubt about it. Video poker machines are a huge success story!

The IGT poker machine pictured here is a special version that will take up to 100 coins! Since the machine will accept so many coins, the payscale appears on the screen, changing in value as each additional coin is inserted. Most poker machines that accept up to 5 coins will have the full payscale listed on the feature-glass at the top of the machine. Notice that the Royal Flush "bonus" increases dramatically as more coins are played, up to 10,000 coins for 100 coins played!

According to the manufacturers, poker machines have gained in popularity because of the skill element involved. As you know, there is no skill associated with conventional reel-type slot machines . . . only luck. With poker, the player has decisions to make. Decisions that can greatly affect his chances of winning.

And there's another important reason for the poker machine's widespread acceptance. It's a proven fact that a great many people like to play poker, but are intimidated by the casino's poker parlors. Some people do not wish to join in at a live game against players they don't know. The poker machine is just that . . . a machine. No intimidation. No apprehension. No strangers. And of course, there are no "tells" to read, and no bluffs to worry about. It's poker, but at the player's own pace, in the player's own world.

HOW TO PLAY

To review the game, the basic rules of poker apply. The "rank of hands" is the same.

The machines are based on a popular poker game called "5-card draw," affording the player an option of drawing up to 5 additional cards. If you're not familiar with draw poker, it's simple.

When you insert your coins, five cards will appear on the 13" color screen. In order to make the best poker hand, you may discard up to five cards and receive that number in new cards which will appear on the screen to make your final hand. If you have a hand that earns a payoff, the machine will do so automatically.

There is no handle to pull; only buttons to push. Since most machines take from 1 to 5 coins, the machine will not display the first five cards until the 5th coin is inserted. If you elect to play less than 5 coins (not recommended), you must "tell" the machine to "deal" (push DEAL button) since it obviously doesn't know if you're just slow putting

RANK OF POKER HANDS
(IN ASCENDING VALUE)

HAND	DESCRIPTION
Jacks-or-Better	Any pair of Jacks, Queens, Kings or Aces.
Two Pair	Two pairs of equal value cards such as two 3's and two 10's.
Three-of-a-Kind	Any three cards of the same value such as three Queens.
Straight	Any five cards in *consecutive* value, not of the same suit, such as 4 of clubs, 5 of hearts, 6 and 7 of spades, and 8 of diamonds.
Flush	Any five cards of the same suit, such as 8, 10, Jack, King, and ace of hearts.
Full House	Five cards that include a pair and three-of-a-kind, such as a pair of Kings and three 10's.
Four-of-a-Kind	Any four cards of the same value (all four cards of the four different suits) such as the 8 of hearts, diamonds, spades, and clubs.
Straight Flush	Any five cards in consecutive value, *of the same suit*, such as 2, 3, 4, 5, and 6 of diamonds.
Royal Flush	*Only* the 10, Jack, Queen, King, and ace *of the same suit*.

It should be noted that the differences in card value is of no consequence to the poker machine player (except single pair "jacks-or-better"). For example, three 2's pays the same as three aces. As a standard poker rule, the ace may count as either high or low in making a straight, A-2-3-4-5, or 10-J-Q-K-A.

in the rest of the coins, or if in fact you are finished betting.

After the five cards appear on your screen, you are now faced with an interesting decision. Which cards will you discard, if any, and which cards should you hold? After making your decision, you simply push the "hold" button that corresponds to each card you wish to keep, and then push the "draw" button. The machine will give you a new card in the place of the ones you discarded. Now, the machine will determine if you have a winning hand, and if so, the machine will pay you according to a pay-scale shown on the machine's feature glass. If you don't have a winning hand, which happens 55% of the time, the machine will simply wait for you to play your next coins.

Incidentally, if you receive a winning hand on the first five cards, such as a straight, flush, four-of-a-kind, or straight flush, be sure to push the hold button for all five cards. Then push "draw" (although you will not receive more cards) to tell the machine you are keeping the initial hand, and get ready for a nice payoff.

To discuss all the possible player strategies for all the possible hands would be somewhat beyond the scope of this beginner's text, however, it should be made clear to the reader that the large jackpot for a royal flush should always be considered a primary goal, and to that end, the player may find that a draw decision clashes somewhat with basic poker strategies. For example, if your hand is Jack, Queen, King of hearts, 10 of spades, and 10 of diamonds, you must discard the pair and go for the royal flush.

Of course, common sense has to apply here also. If your hand is 10 of hearts, 10 of diamonds, 10 of spades, 10 of clubs, and Jack of clubs, don't throw away your four-of-a-kind trying for a royal flush with your 10-Jack of clubs. Use your head! You have plenty of time to think. The machine won't rush you.

Be especially careful with straights. They are rarely

arranged in ascending or descending order, and might be hard to notice. Remember that the ace counts as either high or low in making the straight.

Since virtually all machines pay a 4,000 coin special jackpot for a royal flush with 5 coins inserted (compared to 250 coins for one coin inserted), it behooves the player to insert all five coins. For all other wins, additional coins increase the jackpot by a linear progression — four-of-a-kind pays 25 coins for the first coin, 50 coins for the second coin, 75 coins for the third coin, and so on. But the royal flush pays more than this natural progression for the fifth coin, and accordingly, weighs heavily in the player's overall expectancy. Although the chances of making a royal flush are about 40,000 to 1, these odds should not be considered "out of the realm" especially when compared to the ridiculous millions to 1 odds that the player faces at some reel-type machines.

HOW TO DETERMINE THE PERCENTAGE

What sets poker machines apart from the other reel-type slots is much more than just "player skill." **Perhaps the most important aspect of poker machines is the ability of the player to judge the percentages by a simple review of the pay-scale clearly outlined on all machines.**

Unlike the conventional slot machine, where percentages are hidden in the reel-strips and among over 4,000 programs, poker machines have the same basic "insides" and only a few different pay-scales to rate.

All poker machines are based on a regular 52 card deck, shuffled after 30 to 40 cards are played (some machines shuffle after each deal), so you can correctly assume there are no hidden differences to be worried about, at least not that I'm aware of.

Keeping track of specific cards, as you might do in a live poker game, is not of value to the video poker player because of the automatic and unpredictable shuffling.

To ascertain the machine's percentage of hold, the player only needs to review the pay-scale and look for the most advantageous payouts. Here's a chart that shows four of the popular pay-scales. Notice how significant the percentages change depending on whether or not the machine returns the player's bet (even money) on jacks-or-better.

POPULAR VIDEO POKER PAYTABLES

COINS PAID OUT									PERCENTAGE	
JKs	2PR	3K	ST	FL	FH	4K	SF	RF	W/JKs	W/O JKs
0	1	3	5	6	9	25	50	250	—	66-68%
1	2	3	4	5	6	25	50	250	92-94%	73-75%
1	2	3	4	5	8	25	50	250	93-95%	74-76%
1	2	3	4	6	9	25	50	250	**96-98%**	76-78%

Shown here are four of the more than 50 paytables available, that the player is likely to see in the casino. Note the importance of whether or not the machine pays on Jacks-or-better, nearly 20%! This chart is based on the first coin inserted. 5th coin/royal flush pays 4,000 coins.

From this chart, it can be concluded that the best chance for the player lies with the machine that pays 6 coins for a flush, and 9 coins for a full house. Be sure, however, that 2 pair pays 2 coins. **Indeed, you must be sure that "jacks-or-better" returns your bet!**

Although it's a break even proposition, you should make jacks-or-better over 20% of the time. The casino's advantage goes up over 20% without this important feature. Always look for it!

Player's Skill

Another factor in determining the actual percentage is the degree of player's skill. The percentages found in this chapter are based on average player decisions. Of course, a player could make poor decisions, throwing away straights, breaking up a flush, holding the wrong pair, etc., and could theoretically give the casino a huge advantage. In this case, our pay-scale percentages go out the window.

At the other end however, a player could conceivably achieve a high level of skill and make the right decisions perhaps 99% of the time. In this case (according to Bally), the best pay-scale percentage of 98% could be cut even lower to "98.778%." We're getting "picky" numbers, but at least it's moving in the right direction!

A Dangerous Notion

Since some poker machines feature big progressive jackpots, some authors contend that if the jackpot is large enough, the machine's percentage might actually favor the player! Technically, that might be true, but it's a dangerous notion.

If you are confident that the progressive jackpot is a mathematical certainty in your favor, and you wish to risk literally thousands of coins in pursuit, you must be prepared to lose it all. THERE IS NO GUARANTEE THAT IF YOU WAGER 40,000 TIMES, OR EVEN 100,000 TIMES, THAT YOU WILL LINE UP THE ROYAL FLUSH. NO GUARANTEE WHATSOEVER!

Assuming that in fact you will not make the royal flush, even though it's much "easier" than the million-dollar slot progressives, the poker machine will keep over 4% for the house based on the most favorable pay-scale for the player. That's why we said earlier that the big jackpot counts heavily towards the minimal casino advantage. But you have to win it at least once over the full course of all pro-babilities, and that's a hell of a lot of coins!

Unlike the conventional reel-type progressives, the royal flush jackpot is indeed realistic and should be counted when considering percentages. All I want to make sure you understand is that although 40,000 to 1 is better than 3 million to 1, it's still a major hurdle to clear. It could take a big investment. But then again, it might not.

That's what gambling is all about.

CASH-LESS SLOTS

This is as good a place as any to discuss a new trend in slot machines, including video poker, called "credit-play." Instead of dumping your payoff in the metal coin-tray, a machine might simply hold your winnings until you decide to take them by pushing the "cash-out" button. The problem with this feature is that too many players don't push the cash-out button. They simply play off the credit meter until it shows "0."

It would appear to be better for the player to actually see and feel the coins in your tray to fully appreciate the value of the coins, as opposed to the meter that only displays a number. This problem is analogous to credit at the table games. A player simply asks for a marker and plays it. No cash. Just a piece of paper. In too many cases, credit in the casino is a loaded gun.

Remember, the number of coins displayed on a credit-meter is *your* money, not the machine's money. Take it!

There's another new concept in slot machines underway that will allow the player to use a credit card, instead of actual coins.

The player will apply for the casino-issued credit card at the cashier's cage, and deposit money to play against. To play, you will simply insert the card into the machine, and immediately see on the screen your balance and record of activity. Each time you play and lose, the machine will debit your account. When you win, the machine will credit your account.

Eventually, it's possible that you can use your Master-Card or Visa card to play a slot machine. What next!

"HOT" CHIP!

The photograph on this book's front cover shows a video poker screen with a relatively unexciting display — J-10-4-9-J.

I asked the manufacturer, IGT, to provide a picture of a poker screen displaying the royal flush. At least it would be fun to look at. Frankly, I've never seen one.

The manufacturer's spokesman was quick to point out that it would have taken an "endless number of plays to produce the royal flush, no different than in the casino."

I said, "Come on now, you make the machine. Just set it!"

He replied, "Oh no! It would take a special *hot* chip to automatically produce the royal flush at will. And that would be a dangerous situation — having a special chip floating around that could generate royal flushes on command. We wouldn't make one. It could fall into the wrong hands."

So you see, even the manufacturers can't "adjust" the video machine for a certain combination, nor can the casino.

Unlike the mechanical machines with reels that could be easily set for 7's (also on the book's cover), the video machines are highly sophisticated. In a sense, it would seem they are less vulnerable to manipulation, especially if the actual manufacturers can't even do it!

Incidentally, the next time you line up a royal flush — the hard way, assuming you don't have a "hot" chip — call me so I can take a picture for our next edition.

CHAPTER 9

ANSWERS TO THE MOST COMMONLY ASKED QUESTIONS

WHY IS PICTURE-TAKING PROHIBITED IN THE CASINO?

Perhaps the most common question asked in a casino is "why is picture-taking prohibited?" If a player lines up a nice jackpot, but not big enough to make the newspapers, why can't he at least take a picture to show all his friends back home?

There are several answers to this question, not the least of which is the potential damage a flash can do to the sensitive lenses of the casino's video cameras hidden in and around the casino. The "eye in the sky" keeps a record of activity on all table games and the greater part of the slot machine area. The casino's cameras are usually set for a low light level; a flash from a player's camera might knock them out of focus. Incidentally, the casino's cameras and video-tape machines are there to protect the integrity of the games, for both the casino and the player.

Secondly, one of the casino's major concerns is security. At any given time, there could be millions in cash in and around the casino. It's possible, they suppose, that pictures could help in masterminding a big heist. If that's your reason, you would be smarter taking pictures of Fort Knox. No one in his right mind would consider knocking off a casino.

But the main reason casinos don't allow picture-taking is for the security of their patrons. The casino wishes to protect their players from any embarrassing photographs.

If that high roller whooping it up at the blackjack tables happened to leave his wife back home, yet has two lovely "cousins" on both arms, I would guess the last thing he wants is an 8x10 glossy.

Personally, I like the rule. I don't like the idea of being in someone else's family album, and consider it an invasion of my privacy . . . in the casino or anywhere. Respect the casino's policy and leave your camera in your room. Remember, the casino is a sanctuary for everyone's privacy.

CAN I TAKE MY KIDS INTO THE CASINO?

Another casino policy that many slot players might not know about is actually a Gaming Commission rule prohibiting any person under the age of 21 years to be in the gaming area. Sure, you're 21 and I'm 21 but what if you should decide to take your family to Las Vegas? You can leave the kids in the room with a babysitter only so many times.

Some major hotels offer a child-care service that includes recreational games and treats for the kiddies. But there comes a time when your kids want to "see" the casino.

It's all right to escort your children through the casino, using the main aisles, as long as you continue walking. Don't loiter. If this happens, a security guard will politely tell you to keep moving, and remind you that kids are not allowed in the casino.

I pity the security guards at Circus Circus. Kids love the place. If you've been there, you'll know why.

WILL THE CASINO'S SECURITY CAMERAS PROTECT MY JACKPOTS?

We talked briefly about the casino's security cameras earlier, which reminds me of another common misconception.

Some players think that each slot machine is being visually monitored, and any big win is recorded on tape to identify the player in case there's a dispute. If you hit a big jackpot, it's possible the camera was indeed trained on you, but don't count on it. If you are lucky enough to win a major jackpot (or any jackpot that has to be paid by an attendant), never leave your machine. Tell a change-girl, if you see one, to notify a floorman. Stay with your machine until the floorman comes over to congratulate you. Some floormen are responsible for over 300 machines, so you might have to wait.

Remember, if you hit a big jackpot, or have coins left in the tray, don't leave your machine unattended.

HOW WILL THE CASINO PAY ME IF I WIN?

It's always fun to talk about winning jackpots, so let's stay with the subject. If you do win a big one, how will the casino pay you? It's a bit presumptuous to pin down the casino before you even start to play, so let me tell you. Depending on the size of the jackpot, it's possible that the casino might ask if they can pay you in installments. Twenty thousand a year, fifty thousand a year, not bad! *Of course, you have every right to ask for a check in full!* Unlike a state-run lottery where the winner is paid in yearly installments, and the interest on the unpaid balance pays the installments, you can expect a full check from the casino, even for millions of dollars!

However, your tax accountant might recommend that you take the winnings in installments, and the casino will be happy to oblige!

WILL THE IRS BE NOTIFIED IF I WIN?

On May 1, 1977, an IRS regulation went into effect which requires the casino to report on form W-2G ("G" stands for gambling) all payments on slot winnings of $1,200 or more, and on keno winnings of $1,500 or more.

The IRS considers your winnings as "ordinary income." However, you might be able to deduct your costs for winning that jackpot and other gambling losses that you can substantiate during that year.

When you get home, notify your CPA for professional advice.

WHEN WILL THE CASINO PAY ME IF I WIN?

In the case of a really big jackpot, some casinos may delay payment for a short period — nothing serious, to determine if the win was indeed legitimate. Generally, the machine will be shut down and inspected by the casino's slot-security experts. It's possible the casino will call in an investigator from the Casino Control Commission. They want to be sure, and so would you if it were *your* casino. Instances of slot cheating including million-dollar rip-offs, cost the casino industry over $20 million each year! And they cost the players too. Most casinos build in these losses as part of their sales costs — the percentages we all play against. Cheaters hurt everyone.

So, if you do happen to pull down a biggie, don't take it personal when the casino checks your winning machine (while you watch) with a special micro-chip that when inserted into the machine will display "yes" or "no," yes it's OK, or no, there's a problem. If everything checks out, you might be able to have your check in a few hours. All the casino wants to do is verify that your win was not fraudulent.

WHAT IF I DON'T WANT MY NAME USED FOR PUBLICITY?

The casino's publicity department will probably ask you for permission to use your name and photograph in newspaper and magazine articles, and for their own promotions. You have the right to ask for anonymity. Many players do not wish to have their name released. With all the weirdos running loose, it's not hard to figure why.

WHAT DOES THE CASINO DO IF THEY CATCH A SUSPECTED CHEATER?

While playing slots, there are three things I always recommend that you leave at home: slugs, washers, and your Black & Decker drill.

If a player is caught cheating, he will be escorted by a security guard to a waiting room and detained until the police arrive, or a Gaming Control officer is called. The casino's security guards can detain the suspected cheater but technically cannot arrest him. The police or the Gaming Control agent can and will. It's obviously a serious felony in Nevada and New Jersey and not taken lightly. Even if it's a nickel machine, you're in big trouble.

It's been said that cheating the machines is the only way to beat them. Then consider them unbeatable. Losing a few dollars beats losing a few years.

SHOULD I CONSIDER PLAYING IN A SLOT TOURNAMENT?

Most casino players are aware of the frequent blackjack and craps tournaments sponsored by the big hotels. But did you know that slot tournaments are offered also?

Although the rules vary from casino to casino, basically each player is not only playing against the casino, but against the other players as well. Like poker tournaments, there's a registration requirement and a buy-in of perhaps $200 to $500. Generally, the casino will have special prices for rooms; parties, food, and a special award ceremony for the winners.

For example, the Desert Inn in Las Vegas features several slot tournaments each year with cash and prizes as high as $50,000 with only a $300 buy-in. Generally, the 1st, 2nd, 3rd, and 4th place winners are paid on the basis of entrants in the contest. Slot tournaments are always a lot of fun. To enter, contact your favorite casino and get the facts. Check over the rules and regulations carefully.

CHAPTER 10

GOOD AND BAD ADVICE

There are many popular notions about slot machines that a multitude of players subscribe to . . . axioms and rules that on the surface might sound sensible, but when analyzed, have absolutely no basis of fact. Indeed, it's difficult enough trying to beat the machines without any advice at all, but the wrong advice only makes it twice as tough.

Here are some examples of bad advice, excerpted from the text of other publications widely available on how to beat slot machines.

BAD ADVICE #1. Ask a casino slot attendant which machines are "due" to make a payoff. The attendant may know if the winning jackpot amount has been following a pattern. If you do hit a winner, be sure to tip the attendant.

Sadly, this advice is commonplace, yet totally without merit. First of all, **a slot machine is never "due" for anything. Slot machines are based on the strict laws of random numbers. Every pull of the handle produces an entirely random event, independent of any previous results.** The machines are not keeping track. Nor should you.

If a slot machine has not produced a winning jackpot after 20 pulls, the machine is not "ready" for a jackpot beyond it's natural probability. Do you actually think there's a "force" at work, urging the machine to produce a jackpot because it's overdue? A provocation of mathematical or mechanical energy? It's as ludicrous as it sounds.

Slots are not set by the casino or by the manufacturer to produce a jackpot at a particular time or under particular circumstances. The only basis for the likelihood of that jackpot is its probability. If the odds of a certain jackpot are 499 to 1, then the player should hit it once in 500 pulls. It might be on the first pull, the last pull, or any pull in between.

When I told you that a player should hit the jackpot once in 500 pulls, the important word is "should." Winning the jackpot in 500 pulls is not an absolute. It's an absolute probability. 500 trials represent a relatively short-term test. Anything can happen. Maybe the player will hit the jackpot twice in 500 pulls, maybe three times, maybe not at all . . . even though the odds indicate a win is probable.

Over long-term play, the player will indeed win a jackpot, on average, once in every 500 pulls. That, my friend, is an absolute, and is why the casinos continue to prosper. Long-term, favorable probabilities guarantee the casino a profit every year.

Not only is a slot machine never due at a given point, it never follows a "pattern" either! There is no pattern to random numbers. It's a gross contradiction. "Random" means there is no pattern!

The advice to tip the attendant if you do hit a winner is a nice gesture, but you certainly can't give credit to the attendant. You might as well tip Queen Elizabeth! A "change-girl" has no inside information. The only thing to ask a change-girl for is change!

BAD ADVICE #2. Keep an eye out for a player who's been playing a machine for a long time with no big payoff. When he or she leaves, play that machine.

This advice is pure bunk, for much of the same reasons I cited earlier. Remember, the machine is never "ready" for a payoff. As much as you're going to hate to hear it, the only factor that counts is "luck." You have to be at the right machine at the right time.

Although the author's advice is worthless, even if it did have an ounce of meaning, it's wrong on two counts. If indeed you watched a player pull the handle many times to no avail, the last thing you should want to do is play it! It's possible, although highly unlikely, that a mechanical "bias" in the machine is preventing a jackpot. All casinos monitor slot machines twice a week, looking for any bias that might develop. If the manufacturer designed the machine to hold 5%, that's exactly what the casino wants. Not more. Not less.

Accept the fact that the machine might be on a cold streak (a real mathematical possibility) and find another one.

Just like blackjack or craps, slot machines can produce streaks too. But technically, there's really no such thing as a "hot" or "cold" slot machine; only a machine that *was* hot or *was* cold. At any moment, anyone can tell you their machine *was* hot, not *is* hot. No one can tell you that it will continue. In the random process, streaks are real possibilities. But no one knows when they are about to begin . . . or about to end.

BAD ADVICE #3. The more you play, the more they pay.

I'm not sure what the hell that means, but it makes no sense at all. If you recall from our opening chapter, I gave you the classic rule in the casino for all games: The more you play, the more likely you will lose.

If you're bucking percentages against you, longer play will only enforce that important rule. You're giving the casino's advantage too great a chance of working against you. Hope for short-term triumphs, and give the casino a minimal shot at your money.

The author of that ''bad advice'' we just cited, made matters much worse in the next paragraph by telling the player that if you're winning big on a slot, to reach to the right and to the left and play those adjacent machines also.

Good gosh! Most all astute slot players know that casinos, as a rule, ''mix'' the machine percentages to the extent that a machine beside another might have a different hold. It's possible that identical machines in a row might have holds that vary from 15% to 5%! But more importantly, how could the success of one machine have any real bearing on another? Are they connected by wires? Are they communicating? Will the good fortune of one machine rub off on another? It's the most ridiculous advice I've ever heard of!

Incidentally, the casino's practice of randomly mixing machine percentages throughout the casino seems to be tapering off. At one time, a common recommendation heard from slot experts was to play only the machines at the front entrance or in other high-traffic areas. The theory being that the advertising value of frequent jackpots in conspicuous locations would benefit the casino's *other* machines. A ''come-on'' so to speak. Of course, it was assumed that the ''other'' machines were not as favorable. Some slot experts boldly announced that the machines in the far corners of the casino were set for a higher hold and not worth playing.

Today, in most major casinos, you'll find that the mix of percentages is not that significant, and, in fact, all machines might be set for about the same percentage.

If a casino determines that 10% is the hold they want from the slot department, it's very possible that all machines are set "around" 10%. No big mix. No come-ons. No games.

The casino's reasoning for this new practice centers on the high cost of maintaining the machines. And some casinos offer over a thousand to choose from! Each machine costs the casino about $2,500 per year in taxes, and nearly $500 per year in related, amortized maintenance, inspection, and reporting. More so, each new slot machine costs the casino up to $7,000 to purchase. The last thing a casino wants is a bank of machines that aren't paying their way.

If the word got out that machines in a particular area were set at a higher percentage, the casino would see their investments go down the proverbial tube. Accordingly, most casinos have found that if the percentages are more constant throughout the casino, each machine will carry its own weight.

BAD ADVICE #4. Play nickel machines because your money will last longer.

This advice is questionable, and here's why. A slot machine manufacturer has confirmed to me that **some casinos structure the hold percentage of their machines in respect to the coin value.** This is a little known aspect of slot machines, and a very important one. Unfortunately, it's not a firm rule, but a possibility that must be considered.

For example, nickel machines produce a small volume

of profit for the casino, compared to dollar machines, because the handle is obviously 1/20 to begin with. Where the casino is generally interested only in percentages, here's where they make an exception. Apparently, a bucket full of nickels is no big deal to the casino. A bucket full of dollars . . . well, that's another story! And buckets they are! At the end of each day, security guards open the slot's wooden base and remove buckets of coins that have overflowed the hopper. Buckets and buckets of coins. Which would you rather have, buckets of nickels or buckets of silver dollars?

According to the slot manufacturer, a general assumption about coin-value/hold-percentage ratios is that nickel machines hold from 15% to 20% (Atlantic City cannot exceed 17% by law), quarter machines hold 8% to 12%, and silver dollar machines hold 3% to 5%. Apparently, nickel machines have a higher hold percentage to make up for their "measly" value.

Don't take this advice to the bank because it might not hold true in certain casinos. For example, a few casinos reported to me that their dollar machines held "about" 10%.

When I pressed a casino executive in Northern Nevada about this practice, he responded that ". . . if we don't set our dollar slots for frequent payoffs, they wouldn't see much action." A lot can be read into that statement, but then again, that's just one casino.

No one knows what the percentages really are among the various denomination machines in all the casinos, with the possible exception of the manufacturers, but you certainly couldn't expect them to provide a complete, detailed list. And even if they did, there's no reason to believe that the percentages would remain constant through the years.

As practical advice to the player with three bucks to play with, sure . . . nickel machines will give you more playing time, more pulls, and more fun. But assuming there's some truth to our revelation about coin values, it would make more sense to play a higher denomination machine, if you can afford to do so.

No matter which machine you decide to play, remember that you're fighting a percentage against you. A percentage that, unlike the other casino games, is hard to determine.

But at least we now know that in some cases, especially video poker, slot machines are not really as bad as you might have expected.

Perhaps the best one to play is a big, red machine that hits every time. And all you have to do is pull the tab.

Have fun!